Little Books of Guidance
Finding answers to life's big questions!

Also in the series:
What Do We Mean by 'God'? by Keith Ward
How Do I Pray? by John Pritchard
Why Suffering? by Ian S. Markham
How to Be a Disciple and Digital by Karekin M. Yarian
What Is Christianity? by Rowan Williams
Who Was Jesus? by James D. G. Dunn
Why Go to Church? by C. K. Robertson
How Can Anyone Read the Bible? by L. William Countryman
What Happens When We Die? by Thomas G. Long
What About Sex? by Tobias Stanislas Haller, BSG

WHAT DOES IT MEAN TO BE HOLY WHOLE?

A Little Book of Guidance

TIMOTHY F. SEDGWICK

Church Publishing
NEW YORK

Unless otherwise noted, the Scripture quotations contained herein are from the New Revised Standard Version Bible, copyright © 1989 by the Division of Christian Education of the National Council of Churches of Christ in the U.S.A. Used by permission. All rights reserved.

Church Publishing
19 East 34th Street
New York, NY 10016
www.churchpublishing.org

Cover design by Jennifer Kopec, 2Pug Design
Typeset by Progressive Publishing Services

Library of Congress Cataloging-in-Publication Data

A record of this book is available from the Library of Congress.

ISBN-13: 978-1-64065-021-3 (pbk.)
ISBN-13: 978-1-64065-022-0 (ebook)

Printed in the United States of America

Contents

About the Author   vii

Preface   ix

1 Holy, Holy, Holy   1

2 The Body of the Word   7

3 Conversions   13

4 Remember Me   21

5 Praying   29

6 Holy Living, Holy Dying   37

Notes   45

References and Suggested Readings   47

About the Author

Timothy F. Sedgwick is the Clinton S. Quin Professor of Christian Ethics at Virginia Theological Seminary where he has taught for 21 years and where he served as academic dean for six years. He previously taught at Seabury Western Theological Seminary. This is his sixth book. He has edited two additional books and has written more than fifty professional articles and essays. He earned a Doctor of Philosophy from Vanderbilt University and has served the Episcopal Church on committees, councils, and boards, most recently on the Board of the College for Bishops and as a member of the bi-lateral Anglican-Roman Catholic USA Theological Consultation on Christian ethics and the church. He lives in Alexandria, Virginia.

Preface

This is a book about human memory and the memory of God. I give thanks to Davis Perkins, who then as senior vice president and publisher at Church Publishing, invited me to write a little book for searchers of God, both new and old and both inside and outside the church. This provided me with the opportunity and challenge to write a personal, viewfinder's guide for this search; hence the title, *What Does It Mean to Be Holy Whole?*

Guides are maps. They offer an aerial view of something, and most details are lost from view. This map is no different. Footnotes are the scholarly way of referencing more detailed studies, but as this is a guide, I have only noted direct references. In addition, I have included some suggested readings that offer further directions for exploration. They also point to sources that are the foundation for this guide.

Sources are voices that form conversations. A guide can never do justice to such conversations. It hardly suffices, but the line of the conversation that forms this guide is the Christian tradition and within that the Anglican tradition, especially from Richard Hooker through F.D. Maurice. More specifically, this guide is formed by conversation about what tradition (or traditioning) is; in other words, this guide is a guide to how Christian faith is passed on to others. Robert Bellah, as noted in the recommended readings at the end of chapter two, stands as the contemporary heir of that conversation, which extends back to the work of Emile Durkheim in the sociology of religion and society and forward to Alfred Schutz's phenomenology of the social world. In theology, H. Richard Niebuhr has been central to this conversation in the course of his life and teaching at Yale Divinity School from 1938 to 1962.

Guides take time. It particularly takes time to develop a new guide that makes sense of the old. I am most thankful to Virginia Theological Seminary for its gift of time and support. More broadly, I give thanks to all the saints that have kept company, especially my students over the years, both at VTS and going back to my years teaching at Seabury Western Theological Seminary. We have traveled together. The reward of those travels is immeasurable, not least in hearing how the journey described here has made sense to them and has offered to them a guide in their own journeys.

One person I want to thank individually is David H. Fisher, an Episcopal priest and philosopher of religion. For almost fifty years we have been reading together phenomenology, postmodern thought, and works of all sorts relating religion and culture. Our conversations have shaped these reflections.

My hope is that this guide will serve as a helpful point of entry into the question of what we mean by the term "holy" and, in turn, the quest to be holy. In this way, I hope that this guide will serve as an introduction to the Christian faith.

1

Holy, Holy, Holy

We think of holy people as spiritual seekers, but life is not simply the search for ever-new experience. There is a more fundamental desire to be whole. This is what Christian faith is all about. It takes practice. It takes community. It takes time. It is a life of loss and love, lament, and joy. This is what holiness is all about. Or more simply, this is what Christian faith is all about, a way of life that Christians call grace and salvation.

What is the holy?

Look out to the sea, across the endless prairie, down the river gorge, across mountains, or into the sky and heavens above—the holy comes in the sight, sound, feel, smell, and taste that dawns upon us in such moments. We feel drawn out of ourselves in the vast, immense glory of it all. The old house, our school, the church, the cemetery—these are places that draw us out of ourselves. Physical spaces stir our memories and focus our attention. Some places stir our most intimate memories, while other places bring

1

to mind memories of distant people and times—an aboriginal village, an ancient city, a battlefield, a colosseum, or the footprint of an ancient abbey.

There are some physical locations that are called "thin places." People speak of these as where heaven and earth collide, where you fall from the everyday world into another world. They may be still, but they are not necessarily tranquil. In these places, we are touched in ways that draw us beyond our immediate worries and concerns. We feel connected beyond our selves.

Sometimes we hold a specific object that reminds us of another time and place: the program from a first performance, a drinking mug, a tea bowl, or shells from the seashore. At other times there is a picture, a letter, or a piece of clothing. Objects of all kinds can break the boundaries of time. The old serving dish, hearty meals, and conversations. Backpacks, tents, adventures and expeditions. A prayer book, song book, and choruses of prayer and praise.

Time runs backward as well as forward. We remember stories about our parents, families, friends, heroes, and much more. Think of family pictures of multiple generations, a mother holding her newborn child, sitting next to her mother, with her mother's mother and father standing behind. In these moments, we feel the family gathered together. We feel our bonds with those who have held us fast and who have helped us in turn hold fast to life, those who have lived and died to care for each other. They remind us of all the people who have cared for us—not only our parents and family, not only individuals, but also communities and cultures.

Holy places, holy things, and holy people are given to us in time. With them and in them, we become aware of what has passed. The person we love is not here—they are gone, absent. We lament, and in lamenting, we shudder at our loss. The past is gone, but at the same time, in our loss, in our tears, we remember what was. What we shared is a time and place beyond end, a presence beyond absence. That presence is ineffable; it is larger than words and objects, pictures and sounds. This is the sense of the holy that beckons us and dislocates us.

In his 1917 classic, *The Idea of the Holy,* Rudolph Otto said simply, the holy is the mysterious power that grasps a person, attracts him or her, and makes the person shudder. This is a matter of *mysterium, tremendum, et facinans,* a mystery beyond comprehension that makes us tremble and enchants us.

How is the holy tied to being whole?

The experience of the holy is what psychologist Abraham Maslow spoke of as a "peak experience." In *Towards a Psychology of Being,* Maslow offered descriptions of these experiences by asking people what were their most wonderful, happiest, ecstatic experiences. He was especially interested in how these experiences gave meaning to life. The problem of how to relate peak experiences to the rest of life is as old as human thought about knowing. As the earliest of Greek philosophers, Heraclitus, said, "you can't step into the same river twice."[1] To know something, you have to be able to connect the dots.

Our experience of the world has been compared to a stream—a stream of consciousness. The stream might be said to flow in all directions, or, more likely, our experience of the world ripples and cascades through our consciousness. New experiences in themselves are only moments in time. Where nothing (no-thing) connects, no one thing goes anywhere. It is only by focusing our attention that we can connect one thing to another in some manner or another.

We may make a sketch, take a picture, or make a video that catches the moment, at least from a certain angle. We may tag this moment in words that connect the moment to some larger sense of things—tender care, passionate love, an enduring embrace, a march for justice, an act of mercy, respect by a stranger, or awesome beauty. However, pictures or words that express a larger sense of things aren't themselves holy.

Words themselves serve as images of what endures in what we experience in the moment: love, freedom, beauty, justice, community, the kingdom of God, the will of God, the vision of God, and so forth. To say this another way, peak experiences are holy experiences that connect us beyond ourselves through the images that make sense of our past and form our trust in and hope for the future.

How do we know the holy?

The fourth-century Christian Augustine, bishop of Hippo, has been the most significant thinker in Western Christianity. In his book *Confessions,* he sought to make sense of his life and, in doing so, to make sense of Christianity as a journey into the holy. He called this his conversion or, more literally, the turning of his life around in coming to know God. What he meant by the word "God" is quite simply the mystery of what gives life and endures. At the center of this journey into the holy is memory. As Augustine claims, the mind is memory. How we experience the holy is a matter of memory.

In the first nine chapters of *Confessions,* Augustine describes his spiritual journey. He begins with his experience of time, which is the desire for what connects us to beyond the moment.

What is desired is the holy—not simply a mountain-top experience or an adrenaline rush that leaves one empty and craving another high. "Our heart is restless," he says, "until it rests in you [O God]."[2]

Augustine goes on to describe how his parents desired that he become successful as a powerful speaker and persuasive orator. He became skilled in rhetoric and success gave him access to the opportunities available to those with power. He turned in upon himself. As Augustine writes, "To me it was sweet to love and to be loved . . . I rushed headlong into love . . . My love was returned and in secret I attained the joy that enchains."[3] These acts of love, however, weren't connected to anything beyond himself.

Most tellingly, central to his *Confessions* is Augustine's recounting of stealing pears from an orchard near his home.[4] With a gang of boys, he crept onto the neighbor's land and carried away loads of pears. He says he did not really desire the fruit since he had an abundance of better ones. In fact, as soon as they were plucked, he ate a few and threw the rest to the pigs.

Augustine makes sense of this singular event by asking and remembering what the moment meant as connected to the past and future. The crime alone made the pears tasty. The crime was the pleasure. This might be simply the power of the act—to experience his own power beyond constraint and to have others love and fear him because of his power. His memory, though, also recalled having done harm. And more, he finds that the act made no sense since he didn't desire the fruit and had no reason to harm the owner of the orchard.

This leads Augustine to conclude that he wouldn't have stolen the fruit alone. His desire was the desire to be accepted by his companions: "O friendship most unfriendly, inscrutable seduction of the mind, craving to do harm as a game and a joke, inclination to deprive others arising from no motive of personal gain or of revenge! Someone just says: 'Let's go; let's do it!' and one is ashamed not to be unashamed."[5]

Such singular moments such as stealing the pears were for Augustine moments of absence. To experience the world in the moment is to experience the presence of something and the absence of something more. We experience a desire for something more while we are engaged in an act that is bringing us pleasure. As in the case of Augustine stealing the pears, in our acts we experience our desire for something more, our fault in what we have done, our failure to do something else. The fruit is good. It shouldn't be wasted. Friendship is good, but it isn't about camaraderie formed in random acts of bravado.

Knowing the difference between what connects and what disconnects, what divides and what unites, and what makes sense and what is nonsense requires images that hold and connect the past, present, and future in our memory. As Augustine reflects so eloquently, images aren't reality, but in memory images recall the experience of moments in time so that persons feel and know in the body the unity and fulfillment of desire.

We humans have knowledge of the holy because we can remember. The holy is given in a moment in time. The power of language reveals what it is that unites us in time. Only in time and through time is the holy given. The mystery of the holy is the mystery of time given in the power of the mind as memory.

2

The Body of the Word

We humans remember, imagine, and act because we are language animals. Other animals have languages of their own that we know less about. Humans have language that speaks of the whole and reveals the holy.

What is language? How does language work? These are questions that have been examined from many perspectives. Evolutionary biologists, cultural anthropologists, development psychologists, and neuropsychologists have come to understandings of what language is by looking at how language has developed. In addition, poets, storytellers, linguists, literary critics, comparative literary studies, theologians, and philosophers have come to understand how words work and what they reveal, conceal, and effect.

Language isn't the holy, but language is what connects, describes, and reveals. Language also reveals in disconnecting and silencing. It all begins with "peek-a-boo."

Where does language come from?

Memory begins in the earliest stages of human development, which is evident in a newborn infant. The newborn attaches to the mother's breast and begins to nurse. This is surely hard-wired into humans as it is in all mammals. However, more than stimulus and response—like a plant turning toward the sun—a memory is imprinted in the body of the brain.

An infant cries, recognizes the mother's voice or touch (as distinct from that of a stranger), and turns to the mother. The mother responds and bares her breast; the infant nuzzles and begins to nurse. Here is the beginning of memory, a remembering that is prelinguistic, before words, but nonetheless a language of the body.

By eight to nine months after birth, a baby is able to play peek-a-boo. A mother takes a blanket and holds it up in front of her face. The baby stops smiling. The face is gone. The mother is gone. Suddenly she pulls down the blanket and says, "peek-a-boo." The smile returns. The game is repeated over and over again.

Sometimes the mother pulls the blanket down. Sometimes she looks out from behind the blanket, from one side and then the other. Soon the baby turns her head from side to side, up and down, looking and waiting for where and when the face will appear. After each "peek-a-boo," the baby smiles and squeals with delight, and the mother responds in kind.

This simple game of peek-a-boo is a game of memory following the pattern of gesture, response, and recognition. In her anticipation and response to peek-a-boo, the baby is remembering the one who smiles at and recognizes her. The baby and the adult mirror each other while introducing variations until the memory of each other is of one who recognizes and not simply one who imitates.

This memory of one another is not unique to human beings. The bonding between mother and baby in the broader animal world evidences that humans are not alone in remembering who is mother or father and who is friend or enemy. What is distinctive about human beings is that the language of body gestures that connects persons in time and over time is face to face. Humans look into each other's eyes and speak. In speech language is born.

In speaking, language names some "thing," whether it is an object, a particular pattern in what is happening, or a broader design beyond the particular experience. Beyond peek-a-boo, the word "Mommy" is connected to the many actions of this person called "Mommy." Beyond the game, she is present but also absent, but she will return and be there for good. The associations happen. Connections are made. These may be expressed in the broader development of language. "Mommy loves you. It's okay, I'm right here."

Still further, the experience of this mother may be associated with other mothers. What "Mommy" means beyond the singular moment may then be expressed in a larger identity given in names such as "mothering" or "parenting." And so the word "holy" points to some singular moment but only as it is connected to other moments and reveals a larger sense of things.

How do we get from "mommy" to "holy"?

Language extends what is known beyond immediate, lived experiences. On the one hand, language is a set of signs by which we remember people, places, and things. On the other hand, language draws together words to express broader connections. We can say that words form chains of signification that are woven together in language. From "peek-a-boo" to "Mommy" to "mothering," language makes sense of our lives.

Whether the experience of peek-a-boo, the identification of loving parents, the seasons of the year, or "the holy," words name things and connect things together in some pattern of meaning.

Language is a kind of scaffold building upon the experiences of the moments of our lives. The scaffold connects and creates worlds of meaning. We live in these worlds of meaning. We see differently, connect differently, and act differently than momentary creatures.

Without words, connections are limited to lived experiences. In naming, broader connections are possible. Like the drawing of a figure, we use words to figure out what we have experienced in time: tree, child, sleep, and so forth. And then we connect these images more broadly to express larger connections and other meanings. The experience imaged "as a child I fell asleep under an apple tree" grounds the sense of the image of "the tree of life" with its range of other connections into a broader understanding: "life is a tree that grows from a seed, develops strong roots, and becomes a source of life and shelter."

The scaffolding of language reaches up from peek-a-boo high into the sky to express the broadest patterns of relationships. These may be called ideas or concepts. Time names the experience of change, and space names the experience of the back-sidedness of things, that what we see is extended beyond our immediate perception. We can then reflect that what we know of space is because we experience multiple perceptions of some object tied together in what we refer to as time. And what we know as time is because we see multiple perspectives on things, like the frames that form a picture in a movie.

The scaffold of language, however, is always in danger of reaching too far to where the image is mistaken for reality itself. Language, however, can also reveal that we don't know things as they might be "in themselves." What gives life is not actually a tree. Roots anchor. Hearts fly. Leaves shade. Arms embrace. Language that makes sense is the language of metaphor. That is to say, something is like something else, but it is also not the same.

In Judaism, the kingdom of God is imaged as being like the cedars of Lebanon, magnificent in size and strength. In Christianity, Jesus is remembered as saying the kingdom of God is like a mustard seed that grew and became the place where the birds rested in its branches (Matt. 13:31; Luke 13:19). In reality, the mustard plant is a weedy shrub and not a tree at all. The kingdom of God is not what you first thought, a mighty kingdom towering above all else.

Figure and refigure, deconstruct and reconstruct. The power of language to reveal is also the power to reveal that what you know is more and different than what you think. Language reveals and conceals, but to know more than the moment is to give voice to the moment in language.

Is the holy more than a moment?

As Augustine describes in his *Confessions,*

> What is now evident and clear is that neither future nor past exists, and it is inexact language to speak of three times—past, present, and future. Perhaps it would be exact to say: there are three times: a present of things past, a present of things present, a present of things to come. . . . The present considering the past is the memory, the present considering the present is immediate awareness, the present considering the future is expectation.[6]

Consciousness of one moment in time does not exist apart from memory of the past and expectations for the future. Meaning comes when language connects the lived experiences of the hearers of the word to beyond a moment in time. Through language, the present is experienced in light of the past and as enlightening the future. And so it is in the experience of the holy. The holy points to an experience of a moment in time that makes sense only in terms of what happened before and after the moment.

Most telling about the encounter with the holy are the accounts of vision quests by Native Americans. These are accounts of conversion as boys become young men through a solitary journey in the wilderness. Fasting and with little in the way of shelter, those in quest for a vision are cut off from the ordinary, sustaining life of the community. In the liminal moments of dreams and delirium, visions come in the form of powers beyond the ordinary. The stars dance. The earth cries. Spirits of ancestors speak. Visions rise up. All is quiet. All is alive.

Vision quests are understood as archetypical. Across cultures, the experience of the holy breaks open what life is meant to be. The holy isn't itself the taken-for-granted routine of daily life tied to practical matters: making breakfast, doing dishes, caring for children, making things, trading things, laboring and resting, and so on. The experience of the holy is a different sense of these things, and with that comes a different way of living.

As is common with dreams, a vision quest shakes a person loose from the ordinary. The experience of the sacred must then be integrated into their lives. The meaning of the dream world and its world of spirits may be clear or may require the interpretation of others. In either case, there is a conversion to a new vision of oneself.

The quest for the holy—the vision quest, the pilgrim's quest—is a search, like hounds on a quest for prey. As the quest breaks open the ordinary, it creates another quest, to answer the question, what does the peak experience of the moment mean? Some people have peak experiences of the holy and become holy-seekers in the search for ever new, extraordinary experiences. Other people, like Augustine, become holy. Like Augustine, to know the holy is not for the moment but for the whole of life.

3

Conversions

The stories and images imprinted in our memories shape the quests we embark on and the questions we ask. The conversion to a holy life begins here. Making sense is different depending on where we begin. Our stories and images change, and our lives change, but they aren't invented from scratch.

What story shapes our quest for the holy?

There is no single story or image that shapes our lives. We live in many different communities, each with its own distinct traditions and cultures, from small-scale families to large-scale ethnic and national identities. We work and play in different fields. We have reached the present from many different roads. To use the image developed by Charles Taylor, we live in many different "imaginaries." They overlap, compliment, and conflict.

> Family, ethnic, culture, race.
> Rural, urban, rich, poor.
> Single, gay, young, old.
> Gendered, married, straight.

13

Citizen, patriot, statesman.
Reformer, revolutionary, republican.
Democrat, socialist, liberal.
Conservative, nationalist, cosmopolitan.

Buddhist, Muslim, Hindu, Sikh.
Roman Catholic, Orthodox, Jew.
Amish, Pentecostal, evangelical.
Calvinist, Lutheran, Anglican.
Atheist, spiritual, mystic.

Worker, owner, farmer, clerk.
Manager, banker, miner, maid.
Teacher, builder, lawyer, cook.
Chemist, driver, doctor, priest.

Persons are multicultural. Imaginaries are rich. Memories complement and conflict. Work, friends, and families change over time. Families grow. Friends die. People move. Interests, concerns, cares, and questions change. The world speeds forward in a digital age.

With each disruption of the old in an explosion of possible futures, everything seems liminal, a twilight zone between twilight zones, a day of dawning midnights. In the twilight, persons and groups offer singular images and stories to bind together identities and blunt differences within a group for the sake of solidarity, support, and gain. These are stories of identity politics. Each story is a story of identity for a particular community.

Multiculturalism is itself an identity politic seeking at least tolerance—if not recognition and respect—of differences in order to maximize cooperation for the sake of freedom. These are the new cosmopolitans, usually professional elites for whom the entire world needs to be ordered along the lines of liberal democracy.

But whether cosmopolitans or nationalists, cultures of professional elites or of proletariat communities, social movements or quietist retreats, or simply the variety of religious or quasi-religious communities, the imaginaries of increasing number of persons in the twenty-first century share a common point of view. They share a worldview.

To share a worldview, however, doesn't mean sharing the same view of the world. What they share is the same view *on* the world. The way they remember the past, consider the future, and are focused in the present is the same. They share what has been described since the early twentieth century as a secular worldview.

In a secular view of the world, the story of human life is imaged in terms of freedom and self-fulfillment. Different communities form different cultures. What they share is an overlapping interest for security and prosperity in order to pursue their own lives. These lives are shaped by market economies where all-consuming images convey what to buy and what to do in order to be fulfilled. Where interests diverge and collide, politics is reduced to managing (or failing to manage) those interests. This is the secular world of *realpolitik* where purposes beyond consuming desires are lost from view.

This secular worldview also illumines the challenge in the search for the holy. In a secular age the outlook on the world is instrumental. Everything is a means to an end, and the end is experience itself. Larger purposes and practices aren't taken-for-granted in a way of life as they were in traditional societies.

What is the challenge in the quest for the holy?

In a secular age where cultures are many and overlap, clash, and change, memory is polyphonic. It is given in many sounds, many tones, many rhythms and many chords, in harmonies and dissonance.

In a traditional society where roles and relations are given, replicated from generation to generation, memory is more monophonic.

In a traditional society, peak experiences happen within an established world. They are tied to life transitions within the cycles of life and order of society. Change, choice, and chance are prepared for and celebrated in rituals: rites of passage, initiation, purification, and healing; seasonal rites marking the cycles of the year; hunting rites and ceremonies at the time of planting and harvesting; and blessings of all kinds for all situations.

The experience of the liminal is clear in rites of passage and initiation. In some cultures, girls undergo rites of passage to womanhood at the time of menstruation, just as vision quests have been rites of passage for boys into manhood. Marriage rites, birthing rites, and burial rites: all such rites create the space for those involved to feel the change and challenge of the powers and purposes that move life forward.

Seasonal rituals, such as planting, harvesting, and hunting rituals, similarly mark changes and challenges by turning attention to the powers and purposes that give life. As blessings, these rites give thanks for the order they celebrate and pray that it be so. This is expressed not only in words, but also in symbolic actions. For example, in harvest and hunting rituals, food is blessed and offered in thanksgiving to the spirits or gods as coming from them and by them. Only then is it shared and eaten.

Rituals are the door of entry into the holy. They celebrate change, chance, and challenge while connecting the moment to a larger sense of things, to powers and purposes that create and sustain life beyond ourselves. The liminal experience is tied by ritual to the cycles of life and the cycles of the social order. In the midst of the rite is a peak experience as a deep awareness that attunes a person to the holiness of life as it is given. The holy is experienced as participation in the mysteries of life, living and dying beyond oneself.

Given strong rituals that deeply connect to a way of being in the world, the experience of the holy and the experience of being made whole are inseparable. This is what makes the profane sacred. The powers and purposes that press upon us are holy, good beyond ourselves. The response is participation with reverence and thanksgiving.

Rituals, however, also form prisons. They may consecrate the way things are, and they can bind up the world to make it whole in a set of fixed roles and relations. Life's transitions can become tied to the past glory of the tribe and the promise of its future. The world narrows, and the experience of the holy becomes tied to world maintenance. When rituals imprison, voices outside are not recognized over cries to protect the tribe by ensuring the sacred order of society. The world divides between friend and enemy. The holy is disconnected from the whole.

The divide between the experience of the holy and the order of the world is as old as consciousness of the holy. To mime and name the world beyond the moment is the beginning of consciousness that the holy is given beyond ourselves. This is the mystery that breaks open our world and draws us out beyond ourselves. This is Otto's account of the holy as *mysterium, tremendum et facinans.* At the same time, to mime and name a world beyond the moment is to form an idea of a world that can be conceived as secure. Given the fragility of life, idolatry is born.

The holy challenge is to engage in rituals that reveal the holy without imprisoning the self. In traditional societies, the challenge is to engage in rituals that free the self from imprisonment by society. In a secular world, the challenge is to engage in rituals that reveal a world and free the self from the idea of an absolute freedom that is detached and unbounded.

Traditional societies must loose the holy from the idols of the tribe. Secular societies must bind the holy in ritual practices that connect the holy to the whole of life. To be holy requires rituals that both bind and loose the holy.

How do we bind and loose the holy?

The liminal is at the center of rites of passage and initiation and of seasonal and blessing rituals. At their fullest, rituals effect a consciousness of "not knowing" that gives freedom to consent to a way of life and to change that life. The vision quest, for example, is radicalized in Buddhism to bring about a sense of the holy in the wholeness of life without consecrating the way things are.

In Buddhism, Siddhartha's vision quest is the story of his journey through suffering to the liminal space where the holy is revealed. This quest is centered in meditation where, in silence, the self is experienced as both given in and beyond the web of language.

Images and stories focus attention on daily life. They describe desire in terms of what is needed or wanted in living in time. They hold us captive to perceptions of desire and want. In meditation, however, a person experiences the liminal space between image and consciousness of the self as not defined by or limited by the images we have or the stories we tell. In meditation, images rise in consciousness, but we are loosed from them. They no longer cling to the mind and focus attention on suffering and striving. In meditation, self-striving is shattered.

The ritual practice of meditation is a radicalized ritual process of mindfulness practiced several times a day. Siddhartha is called Buddha—the one whose enlightenment came in a meditative encounter with the holy under a Bohdi tree. In meditation, he came to an awareness of suffering the press of the world but not as self-striving. Therefore, suffering no longer had a claim on the Buddha and could not tie him to what otherwise was an endless death spiral.

Enlightenment for the Buddha didn't lead to escape; rather, it reconciled the self in time. This process leads to a sense of grace and compassion. Such compassion is not a new goal to be achieved. Coming out of mindfulness, out of consciousness of the holy, compassion is a form of attention and presence that moves beyond world maintenance of a given order.

The radical ritual of meditation works to reveal the holy only as it is leads to a way of life in the world. Without practices of life, the radical ritual of meditation centers only on the practice of meditation itself. The challenge in the quest for the holy is two-sided. First, what practices should bind us and draw us into the wholeness of life? Second, what practices should loose us from the roles and relations tied to the strivings of particular societies?

What is required to bind our lives in wholeness and to loose our lives from idolatry is a broader account of the practices that form the self in the experience of the holy as both liminal and incarnate. These are ritual and spiritual practices that form memory, attention, and desire. And these are moral practices that form a life lived in time and eternity. Human communities throughout history are witnesses to this quest. Accounts of these quests are what we call the history of religions.

The Buddha stands at the center of a range of religious communities that has been described as different forms of Buddhism. Other cultures are formed religiously in ways that are distinct and varied—from aboriginal peoples to the rich cultures of China and India to Western culture shaped by forms of Judaism, Christianity, and Islam. For Christians, at the heart of Christian faith are practices of worship that remember Jesus as they celebrate a way of life that follows from the memory of his life and death.

4

Remember Me

The memory of Jesus is for Christians a saving memory. As holy and healing, Christian memories of Jesus began in the gathering of disciples of Jesus. They remembered Jesus as a community of worship shaped by their memory of the Jewish quest for becoming a holy people of God. That memory is polyphonic, made up of many voices heard in worship together with the many voices in Hebrew scripture.

What forms Christian memory?

Hebrew scripture, what Christians have come to call the Old Testament, gathers together in written form the stories, testimonies, teachings, laws, laments, judgments, prayers, and petitions that are central to Jewish memory of the past and expectations for the future. Together these voices form present awareness. They shape attention. At their center, these writings are memories of quests and encounters with the holy centered in the story of Moses and the forming of the Jewish people.

The story of Moses is the story of God's call from the burning bush to lead the Israelites from their slavery in Egypt; a final meal of roasted lamb before escape to freedom in the middle of the night through the Red Sea; wilderness wanderings through the Sinai Peninsula leading to the encounter with God on Mount Sinai and the promulgation of the Ten Commandments; and, at the end of Moses' life, God's call to holiness as a way of life in the midst of promise and judgment, prosperity and destruction.

Different voices in the Hebrew scripture give witness to this journey as the holy mystery of God that claims a people and calls them to make life holy at the risk of life itself. The holiness code of Leviticus; the demand to welcome the stranger; the voice of God not being in the whirlwind but in a still, small voice; the call of the prophets; the psalms and waiting for God; visions of salvation in the midst of destruction; and acclamations that the knowledge of God is beyond human understanding—these are some of the voices that form the memory and expectations that shape vision quests and raise questions that reshape what is imagined.

Christian memory is a Jewish memory, at the center of which is the memory of Jesus as revealing the holy in his life, his teachings, and his death-resurrection. In remembering Jesus, his disciples gathered together as a community of worship, singing, praying, and listening to what had been remembered from the past in hope for the future.

Spoken before they came to be written, stories were told, letters were read, and images—sometimes juxtaposed—were offered. Further, the worshippers shared a life together formed by this memory. They shared meals together, they welcomed guests, they gave thanks, and they prayed for each other given their hopes and concerns.

The early Christian communities were as diverse as the memories they had. In time, some formed what have been called house churches. Others took the path of intentional communities formed around teachers. Those developed and became what were later described as monastic orders. Others were the solitary desert fathers who assumed a separate life of ascetic disciplines regulating food, sleep, prayer, and meditation.

The diversity of Christian memories and hence the diversity of lives witnessing the Christian faith continues. Different communities come together in worship and share their memories and witnesses, and in the midst of their differences, Christians claim a shared identity in common forms of worship, common ways of life, and common beliefs about the Christian faith.

What is central to the memory of Jesus?

Over the first centuries following Jesus' death, common patterns of worship developed, were identified, and then adopted. Most central was the Eucharist as the celebration of Jesus' life, ministry, teaching, and death-resurrection as the fulfillment of the Hebrew memory of the holy quest to be whole. The celebration was tied to the memory of Jesus praying while breaking bread at the Jewish Passover celebration, saying, "This is my body, which is given for you. Do this in remembrance of me" (Luke 22:19; 1 Cor. 11:24).

Those who come to call themselves Christian do so because the memory of Jesus is for them a holy, healing memory. Celebrated in the Eucharist, the memory of Jesus is a radical, ritual process of continued conversion in the encounter of the holy that gives wholeness to life.

Over time, witnesses to this holy and healing life of Jesus as known in the community of worship were written down. These writings were then collected and shared among communities of worship. By the third century after Jesus' death, there was general agreement about twenty-seven written texts that gave voice to the Christian faith. This collection of writings became the New Testament and contains four gospels (Matthew, Mark, Luke, and John), one continuation of a gospel into the life of the early church (Acts of the Apostles), twenty-one letters (from Paul and others), and a vision of the holy cosmos (Revelation).

The witnesses of Hebrew scripture are meant to be read together with the Christian witnesses remembering Jesus. These writings cannot be reduced to a set of claims about definitive events in the past, about a singular set of laws for conduct, or about the absolute nature of God and the universe. They are instead to be read and heard as distinct witnesses so that those in the community of worship can learn about what is holy in order to be holy in their own time and place.

How is the holy given in the memory of Jesus?

The four gospels, the stories of the first followers, letters, and cosmic visions create their own polyphony, especially as they are heard in worship. Different images and stories break down any simple plotting and planning of one's life. Instead, crises—turning points—are told and imaged. They shock, and memory is refigured, awareness is attuned, and expectations are opened.

Memory is refigured when images within writings and between writings are heard together in a new birth of images. The memory of Jesus becomes a holy memory as it attunes those who "have ears to hear" to the holy. That memory is an immediate awareness of grace in the midst of time, a sense of wholeness in the midst of change, and peace of mind as resting and caring in the ordinary.

The memory of Jesus is not univocal—it is not a single voice, a single image, or a single story. Together, worship and hearing the witnesses that form Christian scripture as the Old and New Testaments keep alive the saving memory of Jesus. The crowds who heard Jesus' teachings in the Gospels are remembered as expecting that he would right the world. The new world would be where the blind would see, the lame would walk, and the lost would be found.

The crowds are remembered as thinking that the past would be changed into a new kingdom where the poor would sit down and eat with the rich. They expected that Jesus would be the king of this new kingdom and would lead a march into Jerusalem. And they are remembered as being stunned when instead Jesus was taken away by the authorities, accused of sedition, and killed on a cross with two other outlaws.

The memory of the death of Jesus is the ultimate crisis. Memories of the past and expectations for the future are shocked. Memories are refigured and reconfigured in different ways, not least in the four Gospels.

Mary Magdalene and Mary, the mother of James, come to the tomb the morning after the burial. The angel of the Lord appears and rolls back the stone. The tomb is empty. Jesus is raised from the dead. He is going ahead of his disciples into the wilderness of Galilee where they would see him. The two Marys retreat in terror and amazement and "said nothing to anyone, for they were afraid." End of story (Mark 16:7–8).

Or, they were filled with fear and great joy, run to tell the apostles that he has been raised from the dead and is going ahead to Galilee (Matt. 28:7).

Or they run to tell the apostles but the apostles think this was only an idle tale (Luke 24:11). And then as two of the apostles walk down the road to Emmaus, they talk together about Jesus' life and death and the empty tomb, but they aren't aware of his presence. They don't recognize him. Awareness of his presence doesn't fit their memory of the past and their expectations for the future. Then, over supper their eyes are opened in the breaking of the bread, just as at the last supper before his crucifixion (Luke 24:13–35).

Or Jesus appears to them, breathes on them, and they receive the Holy Spirit (John 20:22). This risen Lord was not a spiritual body, but a human body, body and soul inseparable. Thomas doesn't believe until he puts his hands out and touches Jesus' side (John 20:27–28).

Memories of resurrection and new life are refigured as new connections are made. This memory is given most centrally in the Eucharist. Break bread together. Welcome one another. Give yourself up to another, for another. Love one another. The table around which the Eucharist is celebrated and shared is like any table for sharing a meal together. This same table is the table of a divine banquet in which all of creation is taken and shared together as the gifts of God for the people of God. Jesus' body is the bread broken and shared with all; his blood, the wine, poured out for all.

And so the chain of signification goes on, forward and backward. Those who eat of this bread and drink this wine share in the divine creation. They share in Jesus' death and resurrection. He dwells in them, and they in him. They are made one body in him. As they love and give up themselves, they are given new life.

This is the way, the truth, and the life. This is the Paschal feast, the movement of exodus, the new life of a new people, all people, the people of God. This is the eschatological feast, the celebration of the kingdom of God, here in this body, the body of Christ, already given and not yet as life lived. Here is promise and hope. Here is life eternal. Cross-resurrection. Death-life. Time-eternity.

Again, what is the holy?

God is incarnate and experienced in this play of memory, not as an idea about the purpose and end of things, but as the embodied experience of desire and grace, as already, but not yet. Suffering is reconfigured and connected beyond the experience of the press of the world upon us.

The holy is not the experience that compensates for suffering and loss. The holy is given as suffering and grace together reveal the inseparable nature of time and eternity. This is the healing memory of Christ, given as the experience of the holy revealed in worship that forms a way of life. Cross-resurrection. Paschal mystery. Holy Eucharist. Holy mystery.

This is the encounter with the holy. This is quest and revelation. This is conversion. This is sanctifying the ordinary. This memory is the way of holiness as it attunes us to the world and forms a way of life. We don't cling to what disappears or look ahead to what might appear. Instead, we are present in the midst of time, in the midst of suffering, to the holiness of being.

Again, as Rudolph Otto said, the holy is the mysterious power that grasps a person, attracts him or her, and makes a person shudder. This is a matter of *mysterium tremendum et facinans,* a mystery beyond comprehension that makes us tremble and enchants us. To this we might only add, the holy is the experience of the holiness of being.

5

Praying

A community of worship is a community of memory that celebrates a life lived. In remembering what gives life, the community prays that it might be so. Apart from worship, there is no life lived beyond one moment after another.

Worship takes time. The narrowing of worship to a moment in time, a separate time of a little more than an hour or so once a week, does little more for forming a holy life than no worship at all. But that has not always been so.

What happened to Sunday?

The narrowing of religion to Sunday worship developed alongside the development of a secular age. The connection of the holy to daily life was severed, and the meaning of the holy was narrowed. Instead of a life formed by prayerful worship, the holy became tied to Sunday worship. What happened in focusing religion on Sunday worship is a story that can only be told by looking back before there was any Sunday worship at all.

Since the late nineteenth century, anthropologists have studied Aboriginal peoples for whom anthropologists were the first contact with the "outside" world. During this same time, archeologists recovered ancient texts that offer evidence of the religious worlds of early human societies, perhaps most famously from Egyptian hieroglyphs going back as early as 3200 BCE. Together anthropologists and historians of religion have agreed upon central features of religion, religious ritual, and the meaning of worship.

We might call these early human societies traditional societies. They are traditional in the sense that ritual traditions or practices were woven into the daily rhythms of life. In these rituals, gods or spirits named the powers that animated life. Ritual worship acknowledged and connected to these powers. There were no Sundays.

Rituals have the character of blessings. We say "Bless this food" or "Bless this house." We also say "I have received many blessings" and "I am blessed." In traditional societies, there were ritual blessings of all sorts for all things and offered at all times. Whether for birth or death, becoming a man or a woman, planting and harvesting, or hunting and feasting, rituals were worship as remembering in reverence "what is" and as beseeching in hope for "what is to be."

Setting aside a Sabbath day—in ancient Israel and in Judaism and Christianity—was a ritual response to the deep sense of religion as a practical piety, as a holy way of life. The Sabbath was a day of prayer and practices that remembered and celebrated what was holy and central to daily life. In contrast, in a secular age, all things are measured by what they produce, by what is realized. Instead of deep remembering and celebration of what is—as matters of reverence, thanksgiving, and celebration—worship is judged in terms of whether it is relevant: uplifting, nurturing, inspiring, in short, therapeutic.

Social purposes—such as fellowship, entertainment, pastoral care, education, social service, and political consciousness—have always been served by participation in worship communities. In a secular age, they have become for many the primary reason for church participation. When other opportunities arise to meet these needs, communities of worship become optional, a matter of choice.

What is needed beyond Sunday worship?

Of course, loss of the experience of the holy is not new. This is what religious thinkers have called sin: a false sense of self that turns the self in upon itself, has pride in its own power, and is caught in a narrowing of love to oneself so that reverence and thanksgiving are lost.

Sin as self-love, in fact, seems original, something that comes with the power of becoming conscious of oneself. But the captivity of oneself to one's self-image is heightened in a secular society shaped by a digital age of consumerism. Logarithms send feedback loops of consuming desires. The temptation of idols may have always been present, but in a world saturated in ritual prayer, the idol of the self is at least kept at bay.

An enchanted world where human persons are infused with the powers and purposes of life would be a world before consciousness of the self, before what Christians refer to as "the fall." As the story goes, this is a time in the Garden of Eden before humans become human by eating of the tree of knowledge.

After the fall, the holy breaks our consciousness of self in moments of the unexpected beauty of powers and purposes beyond ourselves. Apart from practices of prayer and worship, however, the holy is only a fleeting moment. Only in practices of prayer and worship is memory formed that attunes persons to the holy in all things.

From their beginnings in the Greek and Roman culture of late antiquity, Christians have developed and called for daily practices of prayer and worship. These are called spiritual practices in the sense that they form the mind, memory, and with that deepen awareness of the holy. Without these, Sunday worship forms a weak memory that is unable to draw human persons into the holy that is life itself.

What are the spiritual practices for a holy life?

Spiritual practices form human awareness and desire. They include bodily disciplines to clear and focus the mind and disciplines of remembering and questioning what has happened and what should be done. Always, though, spiritual practices are about memory. Spiritual practices are grounded in focusing on images and stories, bringing them to mind, and connecting them in recalling what makes sense.

Making sense is bodily as images recall the lived experience of being in the world. Making sense connects one moment to the next in patterns of meaning that resonate in the body. Making sense forms attention to what is significant that shapes human actions.

The chain of signification moving from the memory of the body to patterns, powers, and purposes builds worlds of meaning. For example, the movement from peek-a-boo to the realization that God is love might be imaged as beginning in the recognition in the eye of another and the recognition of being recognized. From there the chain of images develops in concert with a life lived. Embrace. Affirmation. Presence and absence, absence and presence. Care. Consolation. Dependence. Freedom. Fidelity. Trust. Friends. "No one has greater love than this, to lay down one's life for one's friends" (John 15:13). The gift of love. Love and loss, loss and love. Sacrifice and life. Cross-resurrection. God is love.

Spiritual practices are practices of memory. They are holy practices as they form memory of the presence of the holy as the awareness of the mystery that draws us beyond ourselves in the loss of ourselves. Love comes alive in our memory. In holy memory, we are attuned to the holy and called to "love one another" (John 12:12).

As practices of memory, spiritual practices are described in a range of ways. They may be summarized as forms of prayer, confession, contemplation, and meditation.

What is it to pray and to make confession?

In prayer, thanksgiving and beseeching are the focus of memory. As holy memory, prayer begins in thanksgiving and turns outward to the needs that all may be well. Naming blessings turns the self from itself to thanksgiving and praise. In remembering what is good, prayer turns to beseech that it may be so.

Thanksgiving and beseeching attune or join us to God, to the power and purposes beyond ourselves. This is why prayer begins with thanksgiving, for this day and the gift of creation, for food, for those we love and for those who care for us and give us life, and for the opportunities and challenges before us. Expectations are tied to thanksgiving. In giving thanks, our attention is released from a narrow focus on ourselves and turns to the needs of the world about us.

Between thanksgiving and beseeching, we are attuned to suffering. We cry in the midst of the groaning cries of creation, as struggles limit possibilities, as death comes with life. In lament

Christians hear and pray the first words of the Lord's Prayer: "Holy be your name, your kingdom come, your will be done" (Matt. 6:10; Luke 11:2).

Confession is integral to prayer. As in Augustine's *Confessions,* confession is remembering what has been done and what has been left undone, remembering feelings of both joy and sorrow, remembering what is central to a holy life, and remembering that our lives are given beyond our striving. Confession is a turning toward God; in thanksgiving and beseeching, it is a witness to what is a holy life.

What is contemplation and meditation?

To pray is to remember. Contemplation and meditation are basic forms of prayer. The word "meditation" is often used to include the play of imaginative associations and letting go of images in the experience of silence. In the first sense, meditation has been called contemplation. In the second sense, meditation has been called transcendental meditation.

Contemplation is simply holding an image in one's consciousness and letting go of attention to give space to attend more freely, more broadly, and more fully to what is figured in image and word. Contemplation refigures and reconfigures in the play of mirroring the connection to life lived.

For example, the images of love play throughout the history of Christian thought. Stories are told. Images are used. Connections are made and denied. In that play, richer connections are made between stories and images, and between images and contexts and interests.

"Ah, you are beautiful my love . . . You have ravished my heart" (Song of Sol. 1:15, 3:9). Love is beauty. Love is desire. Love is friendship. There is no greater love than giving up oneself for a friend. Love is welcoming the stranger. Love is sacrifice. Cross-resurrection. *Eros, philia, agape.* God is love.

Images subsist in stories. Memory moves from stories told to images given, from images given to stories remembered, and back and forth again and again. The play of language in contemplation is like the scaffolding of signs going up and down from the immediate lived experience to juxtapose, highlight, expand, and contrast patterns of meaning expressing actions, desires, and intended purposes. In such contemplation, attention and awareness are heightened beyond words.

Contemplation can't be understood apart from meditation, at least where meditation is understood as prayerfulness without words. As such, meditation is a mindfulness given in silence. Like the Buddhist meditation, it is a clearing of the mind so that attention is not fixed on images and words where figure and ground are fixed, where stories speak in one voice for all people, where polyphony is silenced. Instead of being caught in the web of images and stories, meditation creates and keeps alive the imaginaries of the mind where the many voices of memory can be heard.

In the polyphony of Christian memory, attention is attuned to time, to love and loss, to care and concern, to fear and hope, to death and life, and to the crucifixion and resurrection. Meditation animates contemplation. Both deepen thanksgiving and beseeching.

What should I do?

Religious communities, such as monastic communities, gather together to pray up to eight times a day. Shaped around thanksgiving and beseeching, the order (or ritual forms) of prayer includes contemplative and meditative practices. Scriptures are read. Psalms and canticles (as verses of praise drawing mostly from scripture) are sung. Often a single line and image are highlighted and used to focus attention and the play of memory. Silence is woven throughout the time of prayer.

These practices of religious communities are imitated on a smaller scale by other Christians. Daily prayer is sometimes done together and sometimes individually. Forms of prayer, contemplation, and meditation vary. Scripture is often read. Music might be sung. Time might be spent in centering prayer, ecstatic prayer, personal witness, and short (or long) reflections on the readings or more generally on Christian faith and life.

Prayer, confession, contemplation, and meditation are also woven into daily life in other ways: in saying grace before meals; in more extended readings; and in examining the day (or days past and the days to come) individually or in conversation with others, in journaling, and in letter writing. As the body is the site of awareness, contemplation and meditation may be tied to bodily disciplines ranging from Eastern meditative practices to regular disciplines of fasting, of work (such as gardening), and of exercise.

Prayer, confession, contemplation, and meditation are ritual practices. They have a consistent pattern. They are countercultural. They take time. They need to happen daily. They may be focused through a retreat lasting a day or several days. Only in this way is memory grounded and deepened in images and stories that make sense of the past, shape expectations, and effect a holy awareness in the present connected to a holy way of life.

6

Holy Living, Holy Dying

For Christians, the quest for the holy is over. In worship, most centrally in the Eucharist, and through spiritual practices, the experience of the holy is now incarnate in memory. Cross-resurrection is the central image of this saving memory of Christ. This is an awareness of the holiness of the whole of life given in invitation and response, thanksgiving and recognition, and reverence and care. This awareness of the holy is to become holy in living a holy life.

Where does holy life begin?

The life of the person begins in recognition. In peek-a-boo, the recognition of recognition is celebrated with glee and delight. Glee and delight are the recognition of life together in time. This life together is a matter of reverence and care.

Other persons to whom I'm drawn toward captivates my attention in all their mystery. I delight in the other, even as I tremble at the mystery of it all. What I revere, I want to be well and to flourish. Reverence and care are twins—to stand in reverence is to respond in care, and to care is to stand in reverence.

Holy living marked by reverence and care is present in everyday life, in our hunting and gathering, travelling and shopping, cooking and serving, washing and cleaning, eating and talking, teaching and learning, playing and singing, and tending and comforting. At the center of this life is the household, and at the center of the household is the table.

Holiness begins by being at table together. Food is shared. Conversations ensue. There is playfulness and seriousness. There are stories to be told, surprises, laughter, recognition of concerns, advice, expressions of support, new questions, other thoughts, and much more. Here is where reverence and care are incarnate. But to make us whole, feasting is more than eating together.

What is feasting?

In traditional nomadic cultures and farming societies, households were tied to the land. Hunting and gathering, planting and harvesting, and going to market with open stalls filled with what others gathered to trade or sell: this insured that food was more than eating. Matters of food were matters of recognition of the natural world, as well as the work of the community.

The fruit of the land were gifts of creation to be recognized with reverence and care. This was done in the manner that the food was gathered, prepared, shared, and eaten. However, these practices all changed with the development of industrialization and the secularization of the modern world.

In contemporary Western societies, and increasingly throughout the world, food is a commodity. Food can be produced and shipped from anywhere to anywhere for the right price. Food is commercialized to create and meet consumer taste. We eat what we want and when we want to. Broken is the connection to the land and to all who share in preparing a feast. The holy is likewise narrowed.

To break the spell of secularization requires incarnating reverence and care beyond eating at the table together. Feasting, for example, includes decisions beginning with how we connect to the land.

> Where to live, how to live,
> what to buy, what to grow?
>
> There is gardening.
> Small garden, large garden, container garden, roof garden;
> vegetable garden, herb garden, flower garden;
> what to seed, what to plant, what to water, what to grow.
>
> There's food buying.
> Going to the market or the store,
> what's in season here and what's abroad.
> Fish or meat, if any at all.
>
> And what to make "from scratch."
> Baking and making, steaming,
> roasting, simmering, stewing.
>
> How to feast. How to eat.
> What to ask. What to say.
> How to thank.

For Christians, this way of life is imaged as the household of God.

What does a holy life require politically?

While every household dwells in creation, every household dwells in society as well. With the table at the center of the household of God, sharing meals together at table is both giving thanks for the gifts of creation and a sharing of those gifts. This feast is given as "gifts of God for the people of God,"[7] as is proclaimed in the Eucharist before the sharing of bread and wine in communion together.

Feasting draws together reverence for creation and the welcome and embrace of strangers as members of one family, a new people, the people of God. However, as a matter of welcome and embrace, as a matter of hospitality, what feasting together requires depends on time and place.

In a nomadic culture, the relationship between households is clear. In carrying their households with them, nomads travel on the path of creation, hunting for and gathering food a day at a time. When strangers are met, hospitality is offered. "Remember," Hebrew scripture says, "you were wandering Arameans" (Deut. 26:5). We depend upon each other. We welcome, give what we can, and then go forward into the wilderness.

The promise of settling on the land to herd and farm is having enough food to eat, plenty enough for families to grow and prosper. The day is, however, no longer sufficient unto itself. You have to plant today in order to harvest tomorrow. You have to store at harvest in order to seed in the spring. The promise carries with it new challenges.

In an agrarian society, households come together to form alliances to trade and to protect each other from those who would steal. Decisions have to be made on how to trade, how to protect each other from enemies within and from without, how to govern, what to require, and what and how to punish. These matters of society are matters of justice. As matters of justice, these are matters of what is fair to each household in order to protect and sustain the households that are bound together.

The development that leads from hunters and gatherers to agrarian societies to industrial and post-industrial societies is the history of collaboration in increasing wealth and opportunities. It is also the history of justice in seeking how to govern and what to govern. With science and technology, collaboration has been woven together on a global scale. This has happened at an exponential rate, doubling and doubling again and again, almost as quickly as the increase in the speed of each generation of computer chips. Wealth has correspondingly increased. So have the challenges of justice.

The promise of a global society is that households will flourish with such collaboration between communities that the threat of enemies will cease. The reality is that inequalities, failed states, and potent terrorists threaten all. In this world, reverence and care for others are in short supply, especially as matters of justice fail to keep pace with society.

Matters of justice in any society are particularly difficult once it is clear that religion as worship, spiritual practices, and moral teachings form a way of life that shapes individual households and their relationships between each other, for good or ill. Decisions must be made about what worship is required, how to provide for worship and teaching, who is to lead and govern, and what dissent is allowed.

The separation of church and state only transfers questions about religion to other parts of life lived together in society. For example, decisions have to be made about what is taught in schools, how to address religious dissent from public policy and civil obligations, and how to govern religious interests in determining public policy.

For Christians, matters of justice are central to a holy life. Reverence and care for others call for welcoming the stranger.

This begins in the household. For Christians, this is expressed in a vision of a final judgment where Jesus says that all are family. To welcome and embrace is to give food to the hungry, something to drink to the thirsty, clothing to the naked, care to the sick, and to visit those in prison (Matt. 25:31–46).

But what welcoming the stranger requires politically as a matter of justice is not clear, for example, in providing aid for natural disasters, in creating refugee centers, in accepting political refugees and others seeking to immigrate, in the use of force in protecting the innocent, and in creating governance where there are only failed states. Given what is possible given limited resources and seemingly infinite needs, the list of moral dilemmas goes on.

What then makes holy life a way of life?

Questions of justice grab our attention. Pictures of suffering call out beyond reasons for why there is such suffering. We may become numb, especially when flooded with images. Or we may be preoccupied with our own concerns or pleasures. But if our memory is attuned in reverence and care, suffering awakens consciousness. We call that consciousness our "conscience." The sense of the holy is stirred. Once again, we are drawn out of ourselves with fear and trembling. We want to solve this fault. But faults open wide and no solution is clear.

In our secular age, "problem solving" is the rule of life. Attention slips from reverence and care and narrows to what can be done. Christian faith becomes a project to be achieved. Christian ethics becomes focused on bringing about the kingdom of God.

Christian faith, however, is not an ethic. In turn, Christian ethics needs to begin with the community of faith in offering an account of the Christian life that will support that life. This will include addressing spiritual and moral practices. It will also seek to enable prayerful reflections and conversations that are central to discern what to do given the possibilities and challenges in life in the world.

A Christian ethic will address specific matters that arise in the course and changes of a lifetime, such as love and desire, sexual relations, friendship, power and authority, roles and relations, education and formation, citizenship, prophetic witness, forgiveness, reconciliation, and vocation. Such reflection, moreover, must address the differences in the ways of living out Christian faith in different communities facing different opportunities and challenges.

Christian ethics is always particular, distinctive for different communities: families raising children and extended families; communities in relatively just societies, communities oppressed by a state and communities in the combat zones of failed states; and monastic communities, new agrarian and self-sustaining communities, peace-making communities renouncing the use of lethal force, and communities in mission and service to others.

Again, a holy life is not an ethic. Christian faith as saving memory is of a different order. Where the holy is revealed in the memory of Christ, attention and expectations are given in the intimate relations of love in the present. What to do is not a project but is discerned at this time and in this place. What we do is best understood as a vocation, a calling given what we discern as our capacities in the midst of possibilities and limitations.

The Christian life is a life of invitation and response, reverence and care, and thanksgiving and beseeching. This life is stretched out in response to the invitation to love in the midst of cries for justice. It can only be lived in the awareness that holy living is holy dying. As a holy life, the Christian life is lived in the memory Christ, celebrated in a community of worship, and lived out in the world. The image of the dance captures the holy character of this life.

Gesture, response, together we dance. Our desire and satisfaction are in the dance. The dance is both intoxicating and soothing. Connected, we are drawn out of ourselves. Connected, we find ourselves. In dancing, we are attuned to each other in reverence and care but only as we are attuned to the music itself. The music of the dance is love. The score is the memory of Jesus. The name of the dance is cross-resurrection. As early Christian writers have written, we participate in the life of God who alone is holy. *Mysterium, tremendum et facinans.*

Notes

1. Heraclitus, *Fragments. The Collected Wisdom of Heraclitus.* tr. Brooks Haxton (NY: Viking Penguin, 2001), fragments 91 and 12.
2. Augustine, *Confessions,* tr. Henry Chadwick (Oxford: Oxford University Press, 1991), Bk. I, chap. i, para. 1, p. 3.
3. Augustine, *Confessions,* tr. Chadwick, III.i.1, p. 35.
4. Augustine, *Confessions,* tr. Chadwick, II.iv–ix, pp. 28–34.
5. Augustine, *Confessions,* tr. Vernon J. Bourke (Washington, D.C.: Catholic University of America Press, 1966), II.ix.17, p. 47.
6. Augustine, *Confessions,* tr. Chadwick, XI.xx.26, p. 235.
7. The Book of Common Prayer (NY: The Church Hymnal Corp., 1986), pp. 338, 364.

References and Suggested Readings

Chapter One

Augustine, Saint. *Confessions*. Tr. Henry Chadwick. Oxford: Oxford University Press, 1991.

Augustine, Saint. *Confessions*. Tr. Vernon J. Bourke. Washington, D.C.: Catholic University of America Press, 1966.

Chapters 1 through 9 are quite short in telling Augustine's story of conversion, which includes his theft of the pears. Chapters 10 through 13 are more expansive in offering his account of time, memory, and the knowledge of God. Throughout, *Confessions* is "confessional." Augustine confesses the story of his search and his faith, especially in the form of prayers.

Maslow, Abraham. *Toward a Psychology of Being*. New York: Van Nostrand-Reinhold, 1968.

Otto, Rudolph. *The Idea of the Holy*. Translated by John W. Harvey. London: Oxford University Press, 1924.

Wolf, Judith. *Heidegger and Theology*. London: Bloomsbury, 2014, as well as the other publications in the Bloomsbury Philosophy and Theology Series.

Much of contemporary philosophy and theology has sought to describe the holy, tied as it is to the human experience of being in time. In Western thought, this work is associated with reflexive philosophy, namely phenomenology. This includes the work of such philosophers as Søren Kierkegaard, Martin Heidegger, Emmanuel Levinas, Simone Weil, Merleau-Ponty, Karl Jasper, Gabriel Marcel, and Paul Ricoeur. Some contemporary theologians that have been most influenced by these thinkers include Karl Barth, Rudolf Bultmann, H. Richard Niebuhr, Paul Tillich, and Karl Rahner. Most notable Anglicans standing in this tradition include Don Cupitt, John Macquarie, Mark McIntosh, John Milbank, Catherine Pickstock, and Rowan Williams.

Buber, Martin. *I and Thou.* Translated by Ronald Gregory Smith. Edinburgh: T. & T. Clark, 1937.

From the tradition of reflexive philosophy, phenomenology, and existentialism, here is a classic, broadly read and popular text addressing the holy as given in the other.

Chapter Two

Bellah, Robert. *Religion in Human Evolution.* Cambridge, MA: The Belknap Press of Harvard University Press, 2011.

This "big book" is the most significant work for understanding how religion develops in society as memory that forms a consciousness of God and a way of life. The book is a "good read," especially if read as several distinct books that are integrally tied into one. Pages 1 to 116 offer an integrated, cross-disciplinary account of the nature of memory and the development of language as fundamentally grounded in ritual. Pages 117 to 264 offer the history of the development of religion from its nomadic origins to the mythopoetics of early civilizations. Pages 265 to 566 provide four distinct histories of the development of the critical awareness of religious faiths across the ancient Israeli, Greek, Chinese, and Indian cultures.

Harrod, Howard L. *Renewing the World. Plains Indian Religion and Morality.* Tucson, AZ: University of Arizona Press, 1987.

This thick account of the rituals, social order, and visions of American Plains Indians gives insight into the liminal movement imaged here as the encounter with the holy in vision quests.

Turner, Victor. *The Ritual Process.* Ithaca, NY: Cornell University Press, 1977.

A classic in anthropology, Turner describes the ritual process in effecting the liminal experience of persons in the process of change in identity.

Chapter Three

Taylor, Charles. *A Secular Age.* Cambridge: The Belknap Press of Harvard University Press, 2007.

This is another "big book" that tells the history of our secular age as arising from and transforming religion in Western culture. In another sense, this is an interlocking collection of essays, each of which can be read on its own and each of which illumines the nature and challenge of the quest for the sacred.

Cayley, David. *North of the Future: The Testament of Ivan Illich as told to David Cayley.* Toronto, CA: House of Anasi Press, 2005.

In these interviews, Illich offers his clearest account of the instrumental thinking central to a secular world. Clear and provocative, Charles Taylor's forward draws on Illich in his contrast between an enchanted world and that of secular society, including Illich's read on the misreading of the parable of the Good Samaritan.

Hesse, Herman. *Siddhartha.* Translated by Hilda Rosner. NY: New Directions, 1951.

Hesse offers a literary account of the Buddha's quest as one that culminates in meditation and enlightenment.

Hanh, Thích Nhất. *The Heart of the Buddha's Teaching.* Berkeley, CA: Parallax Press, 1998.

Thích Nhất Hanh is a Vietnamese Buddhist who formed the community of Plume Village in France. His teachings, collected in more than 100 books, are mostly meditations that provide a rich introduction to Buddhist teachings.

Chapter Four

Lathrop, Gordon W. *Saving Images: The Presence of the Bible in Christian Liturgy.* Minneapolis: Fortress Press, 2017.

Lathrop provides a deep account of Christian memory and the encounter with the holy, grounded in scripture as known in the play of images and texts enacted in worship.

Niebuhr, H. Richard. *The Meaning of Revelation.* Louisville, KY: Westminster John Knox Press, 2003.

This classic study is highly readable as it explores Christian faith as healing memory.

Chapter Five

Classics of Western Spirituality. Mahwah, NJ: Paulist Press.

In a series of more than 150 books, this series offers historical works in spirituality from across Christian traditions as well as from other religions.

Hadot, Pierre. "Spiritual Exercises." In *Philosophy as a Way of Life: Spiritual Exercises from Socrates to Foucault,* edited by Arnold I. Davidson, 81–144. Translated by Michael Case. Malden, MA: Blackwell, 1995.

This chapter introduces the nature of spiritual disciplines in late antiquity and as adopted by Christians.

MacIntosh, Mark. *Mysteries of Faith.* Cambridge, MA: Cowley Publications, 2000.

As one of the books in the Episcopal Church's Teaching Series, MacIntosh describes how Christian memory and the awareness of God are formed in prayer.

Love's Redeeming Work: The Anglican Quest for Holiness, Edited by Geoffrey Rowell, Kenneth Stevenson and Rowan Williams. Oxford: Oxford University Press, 2001.

With short introductions and short selections appropriate for meditation, this is the most comprehensive collection on Anglican spiritual writers.

Saliers, Don E. *Worship as Theology.* Nashville, TN: Abingdon Press, 1994.

This is one of the best introductions to worship and how it forms Christian faith.

Senn, Frank C. *Embodied Liturgy: Lessons in Christian Ritual.* Minneapolis: Fortress Press, 2016.

Given his experience with embodied exercises, Senn explores the connection of the body, memory, and worship.

Daily prayers for morning and evening, along with scriptural readings, are available online from, among many places, The Mission of St. Clare at www.missionstclare.com/english. In addition to websites offering scriptural reflections, broader daily meditations, books, and poetry are significant resources, for example, the many writings of Franciscan Richard Rohr and John S. Dunne, who was a member of the religious Order of the Holy Cross.

Among contemporary Anglicans, see the works of Martin L. Smith, former monk of the Society of St. John the Evangelist (SSJE); e.g., *A Season for the Spirit: Readings for the Days of Lent.* Cambridge, MA: Cowley Publications, 1991.

Chapter Six

Berry, Wendell. *Sex, Economy, Freedom & Community: Eight Essays.* NY: Pantheon Books, 1993.

All the works of Berry offer a vivid account of what it means and what is required to be at home in creation. These essays make explicit how central this is to Christian life.

Davis, Ellen F. *Scripture, Culture, and Agriculture: An Agrarian Reading of the Bible.* New York: Cambridge University Press, 2009.

This reading of scripture offers the most thorough and compelling description of the holiness of life, reverence of the land, and becoming a holy people.

Verhey, Allen. *Remembering Jesus: Christian Community, Scripture, and the Moral Life.* Grand Rapids, MI: W.B. Eerdmans, 2002.

Verhey explores the many voices that form the memory of Jesus and how they inform Christian responses to matters of ethics.

Williams, Rowan. *Being Disciples: Essentials of the Christian Life.* Grand Rapids, MI: Eerdmans, 2016.

A clear and fulsome account of the Christian life that draws together the practice of faith as matters of memory and action.